ADAGIOS
for Organ

Edited by
ROLLIN SMITH

DOVER PUBLICATIONS, INC.
Mineola, New York

Bibliographical Note

This Dover edition, first published in 2007, is a new and original compilation
gathered from early authoritative editions.

International Standard Book Number

ISBN-13: 978-0-486-45734-5
ISBN-10: 0-486-45734-6

Manufactured in the United States by LSC Communications
45734605   2019
www.doverpublications.com

CONTENTS

(Alphabetical by Composer)

Notes on the Music

TOMASO GIOVANNI ALBINONI
Adagio
A self-described "Venetian dilettante," Albinoni was a fine composer whose instrumental music stands between that of Corelli and Vivaldi. In addition to some 48 operas, he composed many concertos; this Adagio is his most popular work.

CHARLES-VALENTIN ALKAN
Prière, Op. 64, No. 5
Charles-Valentin Alkan won first prize in organ at the Paris Conservatoire, yet the only post he ever held was as organist of a synagogue for one month in 1851. Alkan consolidated his keyboard skills by performing publicly on the pedal piano.

The *13 Prières* were published in 1864 and dedicated to the composer's friend Pierre Érard, the piano manufacturer in whose hall he often appeared. They were intended for performance on organ, pedal piano, or piano three-hands.

César Franck regarded Alkan as the "Poet of the Piano." In 1889, the year after Alkan's death, Durand published Franck's arrangement for organ of seven Prières, two Préludes, and one of the harmonium pieces. Franck's choices were those pieces he felt would be most effective for organ performance. While making no essential changes to the music, Franck frequently revised chord spacing, added sustained notes, adjusted the pedal pitches, and made changes to the high treble lines to make them conform to the 54-note compass of the Cavaillé-Coll organ.

CARL PHILIPP EMANUEL BACH
Adagio
Carl Philipp Emanuel Bach was the second of eleven sons of Johann Sebastian and Maria Barbara Bach. Earning a law degree at the age of 24, he abandoned a legal career and devoted himself to music. He was in the service of Frederick the Great for 30 years and in 1768 succeeded Georg Philipp Telemann as music director of the principal churches in Hamburg.

Clock mechanisms that activated organ pipes were popular with the nobility and reached their zenith in the 18th century with original compositions written for them by Handel, Haydn, Mozart, and Beethoven. Frederick the Great was fond of musical clocks and owned several. For them, Bach wrote several miniatures, including this Adagio.

JOHANN SEBASTIAN BACH
"Hark! A Voice Saith, All Are Mortal," BWV 643
The *Little Organ Book* is a collection of 45 chorale préludes intended, like the Inventions, as a method for acquiring technique in organ playing as well as in composition. Albert Schweitzer described it as the dictionary of Bach's musical language. In this funeral chorale prélude the left hand accompaniment is entirely in sixths and thirds while the bass figuration expresses tranquility and reserved joy.

Sigfrid Karg-Elert has edited this version, doubling the rhythm and adding fingering and pedaling.

ÉDOUARD BATISTE
Three Versets, Op. 34
In France, the organist alternated with the choir in performing the sung parts of the Mass and Vespers. The choir sang one verse and the organ played the next. Traditionally, organists based their improvisations of these interludes, or versets, on the Gregorian chant being sung by the choir, but gradually the chant *cantus firmus* was abandoned and replaced with contrasting varied and melodic snippets. One of the more successful and imaginative of the Parisian organists was Édouard Batiste, professor at the Imperial Conservatory and organist of Saint-Eustache. He preserved his improvisational style in *152 Versets, Antiennes and Préludes in All Major and Minor Keys*, Op. 34. In these excerpts Batiste provides a solo on a 4' Flute, an interlude on the 8' foundation stops with a 2b' Nazard added, and a chorus for the Vox Humana.

ARTHUR BIRD
Oriental Sketch No. 2 in F-Minor
Arthur Bird's career spanned the Atlantic, flourishing in Germany as well as in the United States. In the late 1880s, he was considered one of the more promising of the young American orchestral composers and he was the first American to write a major full-length ballet, *Ruebezahl*. The *Three Oriental Sketches*, Op. 41, were composed in 1898 and published in 1903. They evoke a Middle-Eastern atmosphere through use of drones, ostinato bass patterns, open fourths and fifths, chromaticism, and grace note figurations.

LÉON BOËLLMANN
Adagietto, Op. 16, No. 11
A native of Alsace, Léon Boëllmann studied at the École Niedermeyer in Paris and, after winning first prizes in all his subjects by the age of 19, was appointed *organiste-du-chœur*, or choir accompanist, at the Church of Saint-Vincent-de-Paul. In 1887, on the recommendations of Gounod, Délibes, and Cavaillé-Coll, he was appointed organist of the *grand orgue*. His most famous organ work is the *Suite gothique* (in Dover's *Organ Music of French Masters*); his *Douze Pièces*, Op. 16, published five years earlier, remain relatively unknown. The Adagietto is filled with the flowing, charming melodies, colorful harmony, delightful modulations, and expressive counterpoint typical of Boëllmann's works.

ALEXANDRE-P.-F. BOËLY
Adagio non troppo, Op. 14, No. 8
Boëly has been remembered as "The French Bach" because of his devotion to that composer. He was a fine organist and was said to be one of two or three French organists capable of playing

a fugue correctly. He was appointed organist of the Church of Saint-Germain-l'Auxerrois in 1840, but after eleven years of trying to maintain high musical standards in the face of clergy opposition, was dismissed. Boëly was the first organ teacher of Camille Saint-Saëns, who later edited his organ works. This Adagio is from *Douze Morceaux pour l'Orgue Expressif*, Op. 14, composed in 1846.

GIOVANNI BOLZONI
PRELUDIO

Born in Turin, Giovanni Bolzoni was a violinist, orchestral conductor for several opera houses, director of the Turin Conservatory, and a prolific composer in many genres, including the organ. For a time, in 1900, he was Edgar Varèse's harmony and counterpoint teacher. Bolzoni's fame rests on a charming Menuet for strings, Op. 157, long a favorite with the concert-going public.

Preludio, one of Bolzoni's eight organ works, was published in 1900 in a collection of contemporary Italian organ music. Although modestly registered for the Unda maris, it would not be inappropriate to play it with all the strings and celestes coupled together.

JOHANNES BRAHMS
"AH, HOLY JESUS," OP. 122, NO. 2

The *Eleven Chorale Preludes* mark the conclusion of Johannes Brahms's work as a creative artist. This music, together with the *Four Serious Songs,* comprised the whole of the composer's output during the last twelve months of his life.

The tune "Herzliebster Jesus," to which "Ah, holy Jesus, how hast thou offended," is usually sung, was written by Johann Cruger and first published in Berlin in 1640. The text, written ten years earlier, is loosely based on Isaiah 53:4.

GEORGE WHITEFIELD CHADWICK
ELEGY

Upon graduation from the New England Conservatory in 1877, Chadwick spent three years in Germany studying composition and organ—he was one of the first American pupils of Josef Rheinberger. Upon his return to Boston, he taught at the New England Conservatory and became its director in 1897. Horatio Parker was one of Chadwick's first students and when he died at the age of 56, Chadwick paid tribute to him with this deeply moving Elegy.

LOUIS COUPERIN
SARABANDE

Born in Chaumes about 1626, Louis Couperin went to Paris with his teacher, Jacques Chambonnières, around 1650, was organist of Saint-Gervais for a dozen years, and died at the early age of 35. Louis Couperin was the uncle of François Couperin (Le Grand) and the first of eight members of the family, who for 170 successive years were organists of Saint-Gervais in Paris.

The sarabande was a sensuously graceful dance popular in France, Spain, and England in the 16th and 17th centuries. In the classical suite it often served as a slow movement.

H. WALFORD DAVIES
SOLEMN MELODY

In 1898, Davies was appointed organist of London's Temple Church (his assistant for two years was the young Leopold Stokowski). Davies was knighted in 1922 and was appointed organist of St. George's Chapel, Windsor, in 1927. The 1908 *Solemn Melody* is his most famous work and was originally written for organ and strings.

GABRIEL DUPONT
MÉDITATION

Dupont studied with Massenet, Widor, and Vierne at the Paris Conservatoire and became a fine dramatic composer with four published operas. His *Antar* received 40 performances at the Paris Opéra. He suffered from tuberculosis for twelve years, eventually dying at the age of 35. *Méditation* is Dupont's fourth organ work and was published in 1899.

MARCEL DUPRÉ
ANTIPHON III, "I AM BLACK, BUT COMELY," OP. 18, NO. 3

"Nigra sum sed formosa" is the third of five antiphons sung at second vespers on Feasts of the Blessed Virgin Mary. The words are from the Song of Solomon 1:5, "I am black, but comely, O ye daughters of Jerusalem, as the tents of Kedär, as the curtains of Solomon." This antiphon is sung with Psalm 121.

CÉSAR FRANCK
ADAGIO FROM FANTAISIE IN C MAJOR, OP. 16

The Fantaisie in C is the first of César Franck's *Six Pièces* and the 1863 published version is the last of three made by him over a ten-year period. Franck's own metronome marking of T = *c*69 is considerably faster than the usually played T = *c*54. His student, Charles Tournemire, wrote:

The concluding infinitely calm Adagio rejects metronomic rhythm . . . Retrospection . . . contemplation . . . that is the Adagio.

CHRISTOPH WILLIBALD GLUCK
ARIA FROM ORFEO ED EURIDICE

This ravishing Aria is from Gluck's greatest work of the Vienna period, his opera *Orfeo ed Euridice,* premiered on October 5, 1762. A flute solo, it is the B section of the ballet "Dance of the Blessed Spirits" that introduces the second scene of Act II.

ALEXANDRE GUILMANT
MÉDITATION AND ADAGIO, FROM SONATA NO. 6, OP. 86

At the turn of the twentieth century, Félix-Alexandre Guilmant was the most famous organist in the world, not only as a virtuoso (he visited nearly all of the countries of Europe and made three voyages to the United States) but as an improviser, teacher, composer, and music editor. From 1896 until 1911, he was professor of organ at the Paris Conservatoire as well as at the Schola Cantorum, of which he was one of the founders.

Two of Guilmant's beautiful slow movements appear in the Sixth Sonata, completed in September 1897, and dedicated to his colleague Charles-Marie Widor. Guilmant had succeeded Widor at the Paris Conservatoire the previous year.

GEORGE FRIDERIC HANDEL
LARGO FROM XERXES

The ever-popular Largo is an aria from Handel's 1738 opera in which Xerxes, the Persian king, expresses his gratitude for a tree whose branches shade him from the heat of the sun. Its beautiful melody and sustained accompaniment have made it a popular organ transcription for more than two centuries.

VICTOR HERBERT
LARGO, *FROM SYMPHONIC FANTASY FOR THE AEOLIAN ORGAN*

Victor Herbert was the first of several famous contemporary composers commissioned by the Aeolian Organ Company to compose original organ works for their player organs. These works were never published except as perforated paper music rolls, and were sold only to patrons of the company who had an Aeolian Organ in their private residences. The rolls were similar to player piano rolls, except that they played the notes of a two-manual and pedal pipe organ. The "organist" followed instructions printed on the roll to draw the stops and to operate the expression. The perforations have been translated into musical notation by the editor, and we are thus able to recreate a hand-played organ work—the only one to have been composed by Victor Herbert.

Herbert's *Fantasy for Organ* was completed on January 21, 1904. The composition was contemporaneous with his operetta, *Babes in Toyland*, which premiered in Chicago on June 17, 1903. The slow movement, Largo, features an unmistakably instrumental theme by Victor Herbert: the composer at his most melodic.

SIGFRID KARG-ELERT
"DO WITH ME, GOD, ACCORDING TO YOUR GOODNESS," OP. 78, NO. 13

Sigfrid Karg-Elert, successor to Max Reger as professor of composition and theory at the Leipzig Conservatory and one of the most prolific organ composers in the instrument's history, was the first to advance organ composition to the realm of impressionism. His mature style is introspective, harmonically rich, and marked by an almost kaleidoscopic efflorescence of tone colors.

The five verses as well as the melody of "Machs mit mir, Gott," a hymn for the sick and dying, were written by Johann Hermann Schein and published in 1628. Karg-Elert had used the tune previously, treated as a canon at the octave, in *66 Chorale Improvisations*, Op. 65, No. 29.

FRANZ LISZT
AT THE GRAVE OF RICHARD WAGNER

This work was composed on May 22, 1883, the 70th birthday of Richard Wagner, just three months after his death. On the same day Liszt made three different versions: for piano, for string quartet with harp *ad libitum,* and for organ or harmonium.

At the beginning of the manuscript Liszt wrote: "Wagner once reminded me of the similarity between his *Parsifal* motif and my *Excelsior* which was written earlier. . . Let this mention remain here inasmuch as he accomplished the greatness and sublimity of the present art."

Liszt uses the theme of his own *Excelsior* (the first movement of his two-movement work for baritone solo, chorus, and orchestra *The Bells of Strassburg Cathedral*) and ends with the bell motif from Wagner's *Parsifal.*

ALESSANDRO MARCELLO
ADAGIO *FROM* CONCERTO FOR OBOE IN D MINOR

Alessandro Marcello, the brother of Benedetto, was a Venetian nobleman and dilettante who dabbled in the arts—music in particular. His Concerto in D Minor for oboe, strings, and continuo is his best-known work and was transcribed for harpsichord by Johann Sebastian Bach.

FELIX MENDELSSOHN
ADAGIO, *FROM* SONATA IN F MINOR, OP. 65, NO. 1

Mendelssohn composed his *Six Organ Sonatas* at the request of a London publisher acting on the initiative of some English organists who were familiar with his masterly performances on the organ in London and in Birmingham. The Adagio from Sonata No. 1, Op. 65, was composed on December 19, 1844.

GUSTAV MERKEL
TRIO IN CANON *FROM* ORGELSCHULE, OP. 177

A composition student of Robert Schumann, Merkel later studied organ with J. Gottlob Schneider and became professor of organ at the Dresden Conservatory. In addition to nine organ sonatas—all in minor keys—he composed many teaching pieces including an internationally famous *Orgelschule*, Op. 177.

WOLFGANG AMADEUS MOZART
ADAGIO, K. 356

In the mid-18th century it was fashionable to attend concerts performed by rubbing or tapping drinking glasses of various sizes arranged in a row and filled with varying amounts of water. Benjamin Franklin invented an instrument employing 37 glass bowls, graduated in size, mounted end to end on an iron rod or axle so that the whole series revolved uniformly by means of a treadle. The performer sat in front and with fingers moistened and dipped in powdered chalk, lightly touched the rim of the bowl as it revolved.

In the spring of 1791, in the last year of his life, Mozart was inspired to compose for this enchanting instrument. He was commissioned by the blind armonica virtuoso Marianna Kirchgassner to create what was to become his last chamber ensemble composition, the Adagio and Rondo in C, K. 617. This Adagio is a companion piece. Mozart wrote the parts for both hands in the treble clef, keeping the armonica in its most telling range and exploiting its most characteristic sound. The harmonies are delicately colored by chromaticism and inflected with brief ornaments that provide the ineffable grace of the Mozartean style. The ethereal sound of the unaccompanied armonica is best duplicated on the organ with an 8' Flute or Flute Celeste, to which is added a soft Celesta.

GEORGES PONIRIDY
OFFERTOIRE

Georges Poniridy was born in Constantinople of Greek parents. At the age of twenty he won first prize in violin at the Brussels Conservatoire. He was also a pupil of Eugène Ysaÿe. He later studied at the Paris Schola Cantorum under Vincent d'Indy and Albert Roussel. After many years in Europe, Poniridy returned to Greece and eventually became head of the music department of the Greek Ministry of Education in

Athens. He is considered one of the principal representatives of the Greek school. In 1919 Poniridy's only organ work, *Offertoire*, was published.

MAX REGER
MELODIA, OP. 50, NO. 11

A pivotal figure in late German Romantic music, Max Reger was active as an organist, pianist, teacher, theoretician, conductor, and a prodigious composer of music for every conceivable medium. The *Twelve Pieces*, Op. 59, were published in two volumes in 1901.

CAMILLE SAINT-SAËNS
ADAGIO *FROM* SYMPHONY NO. 3 IN C MINOR, OP. 78

As a prodigy, Saint-Saëns was equaled only by Mozart. A brilliant pianist, organist, and composer, he won first prize in organ at the Paris Conservatoire at the age of 16. He was organist of the Church of Saint-Merry (1853–58) and La Madeleine (1858–77), resigning to devote himself to concertizing and composing.

Saint-Saëns conducted the first performance of his Third Symphony in London with the Royal Philharmonic Society in Saint James's Hall, Piccadilly, on May 19, 1886. With this work he climaxed his artistic and creative life. "I have given all that I had to give . . . What I have done I shall never do again."

GUSTAVE SAMAZEUILH
PRÉLUDE

Like C.P.E. Bach, Samazeuilh earned a law degree but then turned his attention to music and studied with Chausson, d'Indy, and Paul Dukas. His musical output was small, and consisted mainly of vocal and instrumental works. He translated *Tristan and Isolde* into French, wrote a study of Paul Dukas, and published a volume of his musical memoirs. Samazeuilh's style is strongly influenced by Debussy but avoids the academic dryness that often characterizes the work of d'Indy's disciples. Prélude, his only organ work, is distinctly impressionistic, and was composed in 1917. Because of the composer's unfamiliarity with the organ, it was registered by its dedicatee, Joseph Bonnet.

ROBERT SCHUMANN
CANON IN B MAJOR, OP. 56, NO. 6

In May 1845, Robert Schumann's wife, Clara, noted in her diary "On April 24 we received a pedalboard to attach beneath the piano, and we had great pleasure from it. Our chief object was to practice organ playing. Robert, however, soon found another interest in the instrument, and composed several *Sketches and Studies for Pedal Piano* that will certainly make a great sensation, being something entirely new." Robert was still working on them through June, and Clara mentioned that she played some of them for Mendelssohn and noted, "It was easy to see how pleased he was."

The six *Studien*, Op. 56, are all in canon form. The sixth, in B major, features the canon on two separate manuals, so each voice is distinct.

CHARLES ALBERT STEBBINS
IN SUMMER

Born in Chicago, Stebbins studied with Wilhelm Middelschulte

and later with Gaston Dethier in New York. For over 30 years he was the Chicago representative for the Aeolian Organ Company.

In Summer, published in 1905, became a popular recital work and was recorded for the Welte player organ by the great Canadian organist Lynnwood Farnam. "A Short Sketch for Organ," it is descriptive of the composer's original verse.

GUSTAV ADOLPH THOMAS
TRIO ON "O SACRED HEAD SURROUNDED," *FROM SIX CHORALE TRIOS*, OP. 7, NO. 1

Thomas studied at the Leipzig Conservatory and was for many years organist of the Reformed Church in Leipzig. In 1866 he succeeded Heinrich Stiehl as organist of St. Peter's Church in St. Petersburg, Russia, but died four years later at the age of 28. The Trio on "O Sacred Head Surrounded" is the first of his *Six Chorale Trios* published in 1865.

CHARLES TOURNEMIRE
LARGHETTO, *FROM DIX PIÈCES EN STYLE LIBRE*, OP. 21

Charles Tournemire had been an organ student of César Franck and Charles-Marie Widor at the Paris Conservatoire, and in 1898 he succeeded Gabriel Pierné as organist of Sainte-Clotilde in Paris.

This Larghetto is the fourth of *Ten Pieces in Free Style* composed in 1901–2. It is dedicated to the then-17-year-old Joseph Bonnet, Tournemire's organ student, who would win a first prize in Guilmant's organ class at the Conservatoire in 1904.

LOUIS VIERNE
PRÉLUDE FUNÈBRE, OP. 4

In spite of such poor eyesight that he was educated in a school for the blind, Louis Vierne won a first prize in organ at the Paris Conservatoire, where he studied with César Franck and Charles-Marie Widor, and in 1900 was appointed organist of Notre-Dame Cathedral. He remained at this post until his death at the console during an organ recital in June 1937. The *Prélude Funèbre* was published in 1896 in the eighth volume of Widor's series *L'Orgue Moderne*. It is unmistakably in Vierne's early style and foreshadows the first movement of his first symphony.

ANTONIO VIVALDI
LARGO, *FROM* CONCERTO IN B♭ MAJOR, "LA STRAVAGANZA," OP. 4, NO. 1

The Concerto in B-flat for violin, strings, and continuo is the first of the set of Opus 4, known as "La Stravaganza," noted for its harmonic daring and its new solo-concerto form, which was to become so typical of the composer. This Largo, the second movement, is an extraordinarily beautiful extended violin solo; most slow movements of the period were little more than a few chords.

SAMUEL WESLEY
LARGHETTO *FROM* VOLUNTARY IN G MINOR, OP. 6, NO. 9

Samuel Wesley was the son of Charles, the hymn writer, nephew of John, the founder of Methodism, and father of

Samuel Sebastian. He began his musical career as a child prodigy and became the greatest English organist of his generation. Wesley was one of the first to promote the music of J.S. Bach in England, and in 1813 published an edition of the *Well-Tempered Clavier*. The Voluntary in G Minor, essentially a prélude and fugue, was composed between 1806 and 1810.

SAMUEL SEBASTIAN WESLEY
LARGHETTO IN F# MINOR

Samuel Sebastian Wesley was one of the seven illegitimate sons of Samuel Wesley by his housekeeper. He became one of the premier figures in 19th-century English church music but was a difficult personality and held many posts for short periods. He was organist of Hereford and Exeter cathedrals and of Gloucester Cathedral for eleven years until his death in 1876.

While his organ works are not as well known as his anthems, the Larghetto in F-sharp Minor, published posthumously, has remained in the repertoire.

CHARLES-MARIE WIDOR
ADAGIO *FROM* SYMPHONIE NO. 5, OP. 42-1

Within two years of succeeding Lefébure-Wély in 1870 as organist of Saint-Sulpice, where he presided over the largest organ in France, Charles-Marie Widor published his first four organ symphonies. Consisting of five to seven movements, they exploit the symphonic instruments of the French organbuilder Aristide Cavaillé-Coll to the ultimate degree. Widor first played his Fifth Symphony at the Trocadéro on Sunday, October 19, 1879.

ROLLIN SMITH

SARABANDE

LOUIS COUPERIN
1626–1661

ADAGIO
from Concerto for Oboe in D Minor

Transcribed by JOHANN SEBASTIAN BACH

ALESSANDRO MARCELLO
1669–1747

ADAGIO

Transcribed by ROLLIN SMITH

TOMASO GIOVANNI ALBINONI
1671–1751

a sua eccellenza il Sig. Vettor Delfino

LARGO
from Concerto in B♭ Major, "La Stravaganza," Op. 4, No. 1

Transcribed by ROLLIN SMITH

ANTONIO VIVALDI
1678–1741

HARK! A VOICE SAITH, ALL ARE MORTAL

Alle menschen müsen sterben, BWV 643

SWELL: Solo stop 8'
CHOIR: Dulciana 8'
PEDAL: p, Choir to Pedal

JOHANN SEBASTIAN BACH
1685–1750

Notated and Edited by SIGFRID KARG-ELERT

LARGO

from *Xerxes*

Arranged by ROLLIN SMITH

GEORGE FRIDERIC HANDEL
1685–1759

ADAGIO

CARL PHILIPP EMANUEL BACH
1714–1788

ARIA

from *Orfeo ed Euridice*

I: Solo or Solo combination. Tremolo ad lib.
II: Soft accompaniment
PEDAL: Soft 16', II to Pedal

CHRISTOPH WILLIBALD GLUCK
1714–1787

Transcribed by Edward Shippen Barnes

ADAGIO

K. 356

WOLFGANG AMADEUS MOZART
1756–1791

LARGHETTO

from Voluntary in G Minor, Op. 6, No. 9

I: 8' Diapason and Stopped Diapason
II: 8' Flute and/or Dulciana

SAMUEL WESLEY
1766–1837

Stopped Diapason Bass

à Monsieur le Marquis de Corberon

ADAGIO NON TROPPO

Op. 14, No. 8

ALEXANDRE-P.-F. BOËLY
1785–1858

AT THE GRAVE OF RICHARD WAGNER

FRANZ LISZT
1811–1886

ADAGIO

from Sonata in F Minor, Op. 65, No. 1

FELIX MENDELSSOHN
1809–1847

LARGHETTO IN F# MINOR

SWELL: 8' Oboe
GREAT: 8' Flute
CHOIR: 8' Dulciana
PEDAL: soft 16'

SAMUEL SEBASTIAN WESLEY
1810–1876

*) Note: This passage can also be played (8va) on the Swell with Contra Fagotta 16', and Flute 4'.

CANON IN B MAJOR

Op. 56, No. 6

SWELL: Salicional 8', Voix céleste 8', Flute 8'
GREAT: No stops. Swell & Choir to Great
CHOIR: Concert Flute 8', Dulciana 8', Geigenprincipal 8' or Gamba 8'

ROBERT SCHUMANN
1810–1856

Edited by JOSEPH BONNET

off Sw. to Ped.

à la mémoire de Pierre Erard

PRIÈRE
Op. 64, No. 5

R: Jeux de fonds et Jeux d'anches
P: Flûte et Bourdon de 8 pieds
G.-O: Jeux de fonds de 8 pieds
Péd: Jeux de fonds de 8 et de 16 pieds
          Tirasse du P. Claviers accouplés

CHARLES-VALENTIN ALKAN
1813–1888

Arranged for Organ by CÉSAR FRANCK

42

à mon Fils Georges, à ma Fille Berthe

THREE VERSETS, Op. 34
RÉCIT DE FLÛTE HARMONIQUE DE 4
Op. 34, No. 115

RÉCIT: *Flûte harmonique* de 4
POSITIF: Fonds doux de 8 pieds

ÉDOUARD BATISTE
1820–1876

à mon Fils Georges, à ma Fille Berthe

THREE VERSETS, Op. 34
VERSET POUR TOUS LES FONDS ET UN NAZARD
Op. 34, No. 56

RÉCIT: *Voix humaine, Bourdon* de 8, *Flûte harmonique* de 8, *et Tremblant*

ÉDOUARD BATISTE
1820–1876

à mon Fils Georges, à ma Fille Berthe

THREE VERSETS, Op. 34

CHŒUR DE VOIX HUMAINE

Op. 34, No. 79

Gd.-ORGUE: Tous les Fonds et un *Nazard*

ÉDOUARD BATISTE
1820–1876

à la mémoire de Franz Liszt

ADAGIO

from Symphony No. 3 in C Minor, Op. 78

RÉCIT: Hautbois, Flûte & Gambe 8
POSITIF: Jeux doux de 8
Gd.-ORGUE: Flûte harmonique de 8
PÉDALE: Bourdons 16, Flûte de 8

CAMILLE SAINT-SAËNS
1835–1921

Transcribed by ÉMILE BERNARD

G.O.
Gt

RÉC.
SW.

Otez Hautbois, ajoutez Voix céleste
Oboe in, add. Vox angelica

POS.
CH.

REC. Ôtez Voix céleste, ajoutez Hautbois
SW. *Vox angelica in, add. Oboe*

POS.
CH.

Voix céleste, ôtez le Hautbois
Oboe in. add. Vox angelica

POS.
CH.

REC.
SW.   Flûte 8 et 4. Ôtez Voix céleste
Vox angelica inn.

pp legato

G.O. Flûte douce et Bourdon de 8 p.
Gt Flute & stop diapason 8

poco cresc.

pp

G.O.
G^t

sf

RÉC. ajoutez Gambe de 8
SW. add. Viola di gamba 8

cresc.

A son ami Monsieur Alexis Chauvet

ADAGIO

from Fantaisie in C Major, Op. 16

RÉCIT: Voix humaine, Bourdon, Flûte et Gambe de 8 pieds
POSITIF: Bourdon de 16
PÉDALE: Bourdon de 16, 8 et 32
Accouplement du **R**. au **P**.

CÉSAR FRANCK
1822–1890

AH! HOLY JESUS

HERZLIEBSTER JESU

Op. 122, No. 2

JOHANNES BRAHMS
1833–1897

Beloved Jesus, what was Thine offense, that man hath pronounced so harsh a judgment?
What Thy guilt? What Thy wrongdoings?

TRIO IN CANON

from *Orgelschule,* Op. 177

GUSTAV MERKEL
1827–1886

à mon ami Charles-Marie Widor

MÉDITATION
from Sonata No. 6, Op. 86

RÉCIT: Bourdon et Gambe (ou Diapason) de 8 P.
POS. et **Gd.-O.:** réunis. Bourdon et Fl. Harm. de 8 P.
PÉDALE: Soubasse de 16, Bourdon et Flûte de 8 P.

ALEXANDRE GUILMANT
1837–1911

à mon ami Charles-Marie Widor

ADAGIO
from Sonata No. 6, Op. 86

RÉCIT: Voix Céleste de P.
POSITIF: Unda maris de 8 P. Récit accouplé.
Gd-ORGUE: Gambe et Bourdon. de 8 P. Récit et Pos. accouplés.
PÉDALE: Bourdons 32, 16 et 8 P. Tirasse du Récit.

ALEXANDRE GUILMANT
1837–1911

PRELUDIO

MANUAL: Unda Maris
PÉDALE: 16' and 8'

GIOVANNI BOLZONI
1841–1919

Herrn Dr. R. Papperitz
Lehrer am Conservatorium der Music zu Leipzig

TRIO ON
"O SACRED HEAD SURROUNDED"

from *Six Chorale Trios,* Op. 7, No. 1

GUSTAV ADOLPH THOMAS
1842–1870

ADAGIO
from Symphonie No. 5, Op. 42-1

RÉCIT: Gambe et Voix céleste
Gd-ORGUE: Fonds de 8, 16
PÉDALE: Flûte 4

CHARLES-MARIE WIDOR
1844–1937

IN MEMORIAM
For Horatio Parker

ELEGY

SWELL: 8 ft. String & Flute, coupled to Choir and Great
CHOIR: 8 ft. and soft reed, coupled to Great
GREAT: 8 ft. String & Flute
PEDAL: 16 ft. & 8 ft.

GEORGE WHITEFIELD CHADWICK
1854–1931

ORIENTAL SKETCH NO. 2
in F Minor

ECHO: Unda Maris 8'
SWELL: Oboe, Flute 4', Trem.
GREAT: Flute, small Diapason, Gamba 8'
CHOIR: Violin Diapason 8', Flutes 8' & 4'
PEDAL: Very soft 16' string, Echo to Pedal

ARTHUR BIRD
1856–1923

Registration by S. ARCHER GIBSON

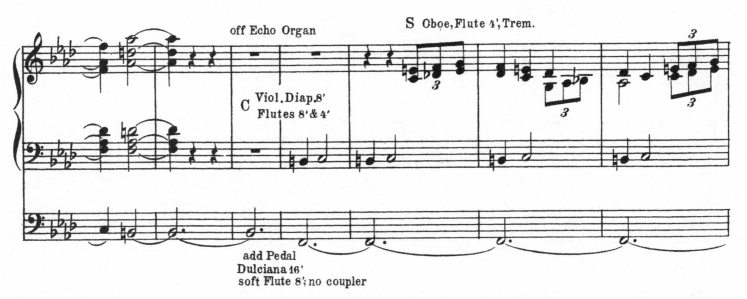

À mon Ami OCTAVE BOUAULT, Organiste de la Cathédrale de Monaco

ADAGIETTO
Op. 16, No. 11

Gd.-ORGUE: 8' Flûte
RÉCIT: Voix céleste 8' coupled to Grand-Orgue
PÉDALE: 16' & 8' Basses

LÉON BOËLLMANN
1862–1897

LARGO

from *Symphonic Fantasy for the Aeolian Organ*

SWELL: Soft String, Vox Humana, 8' Bourdon, and Tremolo
GREAT: Strings and Celestes all coupled to Great

VICTOR HERBERT
1859–1924

SOLEMN MELODY

Arranged by JOHN E. WEST

H. WALFORD DAVIES
1869–1941

à la Mémoire de Monsieur l'Abbé LEVASSEUR

PRÉLUDE FUNÈBRE

Op. 4

Gd-ORGUE: Fonds 8.
POSITIF: Flûte, Bourdon, Salicional 8.
RÉCIT: Fonds 8.
PÉDALE: Fonds 8, 16.

LOUIS VIERNE
1870–1937

MELODIA
Op. 50, No. 11

MAX REGER
1873–1916

à Joseph Bonnet

LARGHETTO
from *Dix Pièces en style libre*, Op. 21

RÉCIT: Gambe et Voix Céleste

CHARLES TOURNEMIRE
1870–1939

IN SUMMER

The plaintive piping of God Pan
Floats through the shimmering haze;
The lazy, far-off hillsides doze,
And dream of other days,
Till joyous youths of Arcady
Sweep by in sunburnt rout
and leave the listening leafy trees
Drunk with their golden shout.

CHARLES ALBERT STEBBINS
1874–1958

Very softly and mysteriously
Sw. Aeoline *trem.*

soft 16′ coup. to Swell

* Accompanimental Arpeggios on the Harp *ad libitum*

MACHS MIT MIR, GOTT

Do With Me, God, According To Your Goodness

Op. 78, No. 13

II: Soft 8' & 4' stops
III: 8' Vox Celeste
PEDAL: 4' only

SIGFRID KARG-ELERT
1877–1933

Con gran espressione. Divotamente. M.M. ♩= 48

PRÉLUDE

RÉCIT: Gambe 8 seule (ou Gambe 8 et Quintaton 8). Préparez Trompette 8.
POSITIF: Flûte 8, Bourdon 8. Récit accouplé.
Gd.-ORGUE: Flûte, Bourdon, Salicional 8. Récit et Pos. accouplés.
PÉDALE: Soubasse 16, Bourdon 8.

GUSTAVE SAMAZEUILH
1877–1967

Registration by JOSEPH BONNET

MÉDITATION

Gd-ORGUE: 8' Flûte harmonique
RÉCIT: 8' Voix célestes
PÉDALE: 8' Flute
Tirasse Récit

GABRIEL DUPONT
1878–1914

113

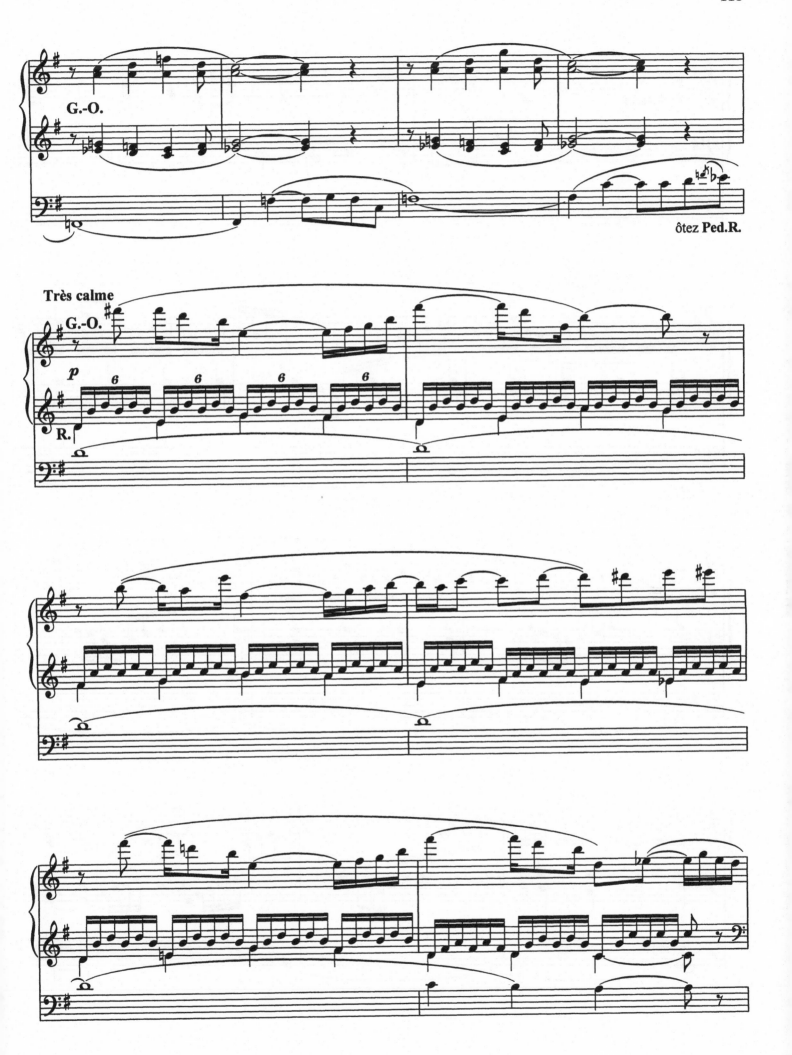

+16'

to Claude Johnson

ANTIPHON III
I Am Black, But Comely, O Ye Daughters Of Jerusalem
Op. 18, No. 3

Gd.-ORGUE: 8' Flûte harmonique
RÉCIT: 16' Quintaton et 8' Voix célestes
PÉDALE: 32' 16' & 8' Bourdons

MARCEL DUPRÉ
1886–1971

Très lent et sans rigueur. **(Very slowly and in free time.)**

OFFERTOIRE

GEORGES PONIRIDY
1892–1982